Daniel Handler

The Real Lemony Snicket

Daniel Handler

The Real Lemony Snicket

Hayley Mitchell Haugen

KIDHAVEN PRESS

An imprint of Thomson Gale, a part of The Thomson Corporation

THOMSON

GALE

Detroit • New York • San Francisco • San Diego • New Haven, Conn. • Waterville, Maine • London • Munich

THOMSON

™

FITZGERALD SCHOOL<del>GALE</del>
Library/Media Center

Daniel Handler : the real Lemon

LIBRARY OF CONGRESS CATALOGING-IN-PUBLICATION DATA

Haugen, Hayley Mitchell, 1968–
Daniel Handler: The Real Lemony Snicket / by Hayley Mitchell Haugen.
p. cm. — (Inventors and creators)
Includes bibliographical references and index.
ISBN 0-7377-3117-6 (hardcover : alk. paper)
1. Snicket, Lemony. Series of unfortunate events—Juvenile literature. 2. Children's stories, American—History and criticism—Juvenile literature. 3. Children's stories—Authorship—Juvenile literature. I. Title. II. Series.
PS3558.A4636Z68 2005
813'.54—dc22
2004024873

Contents

The Most Dreadful Books

L emony Snicket is the author of the children's book series, A Series of Unfortunate Events. As the title suggests, the novels in this series are not happy ones. In fact, on the back of every book jacket, Lemony Snicket warns young readers against reading his books. For instance, on the back of *The Hostile Hospital,* he cautions, "There are many pleasant things to read about, but this book contains none of them."[1]

Should readers ignore Snicket's advice and venture into the series, they meet the Baudelaire orphans. Violet, fourteen, is an inventor. Twelve-year-old Klaus is an intellectual with a knack for reading and learning new words. Baby Sunny is an infant with four very sharp teeth. After their parents die in a house fire, the Baudelaire children must fight to save themselves and their family fortune. Their archenemy is the evil Count Olaf, who relentlessly pursues them and makes their lives miserable.

Snicket's books contain no morals, few carefree moments, and no happy endings. In spite of this—and many would say because of this—A Series of Unfortunate Events is currently one of the most popular children's book series in the world. In September 2001, Lemony Snicket had five books on the *New York Times'* children's best-seller list. Three years later, in September 2004, over 25 million copies of the books had sold worldwide. The series has been translated into thirty languages.

Lemony Snicket loves to sign autographs for the many fans of his children's book series, A Series of Unfortunate Events.

These young fans are very excited to meet Lemony Snicket at a 2004 book signing.

Lemony Snicket's books still fly off the shelves in bookstores the minute they are published. The December 2004 release of the movie version of A Series of Unfortunate Events added to the enthusiasm of Snicket fans. The books and movie have made Snicket a multimillionaire before age thirty-two. It is not his millions, however, that make him an interesting inventor and creator. Rather, it is the fact that when Snicket's young readers grow up, they will remember the books they adored by an author who changed the face of children's literature.

Chapter One

The Real
Lemony Snicket

W ho exactly is Lemony Snicket? Aside from being the author and narrator of A Series of Unfortunate Events, he is also known to some as Daniel Handler. Daniel Handler was born in San Francisco in 1970. His mother, Sandra Handler, is the dean of behavioral sciences at the City College of San Francisco. His father, Lou Handler, is a certified public accountant. According to his mother, Handler's childhood in San Francisco was fairly ordinary. He was a gifted and popular student at Hoover Middle School. His classmates voted him "best personality," "friendliest," and "class clown" for the school yearbook.

In his free time, Handler often rode bikes with friends. He also enjoyed music. He took piano lessons as a child and in high school learned to play the accordion and the tuba. Handler took an interest in acting too. As a student at Lowell High School, he acted in plays such as *Harvey,* by playwright Mary Chase, and Shakespeare's *A Midsummer Night's Dream.*

As a child, Daniel Handler learned to play the accordion, and he still loves to perform for his fans.

As much as Handler enjoyed acting and music, the books he read as a child influenced his writing more than anything else. Handler's father has noted that even when Daniel was a child, he did not like to read children's books that had predictable endings. If he came across a book in which all the characters lived happily ever after, he would toss it aside, annoyed at having spent time reading it. He also liked books in which scary things happened to the characters. These were not things he had experienced himself during his very normal childhood. Handler says, "I have always preferred stories in which mysterious and creepy things happen. As a kid, I hated books where everyone joined the softball team and had a grand time or found true love on a picnic. I liked stories set in an eerie castle that was invaded by a snake that strangled the residents."[2]

Count Olaf, pictured in the 2004 movie based on Snicket's books, is the kind of creepy character the young Handler loved to read about.

Handler enjoyed books by Roald Dahl and Edward Gorey. He liked that their young characters usually got into sticky situations and had to find ways out of those situation by themselves. He did not enjoy books about boys and sports that seemed to be so popular with other boys his age. Handler's mother says this makes sense to her. Handler was never all that interested in sports. He would often allow balls to roll right past him on the field as he inspected bugs during his soccer games.

Handler's parents helped instill a love of books in him as a child. When reading to him at night, his parents would often stop at suspenseful moments and tell him he would have to wait until the next night to hear the rest. They warned him that under no circumstances should he turn on the light and continue reading once they left the room. This tactic of raising a story's suspense to almost unbearable heights encouraged Daniel to continue reading his books deep into the night. It also became a technique he used later when writing A Series of Unfortunate Events.

Handler Before Snicket

Between his childhood and becoming a successful children's author, Handler's life progressed along in a fairly typical way. After graduating from Lowell High School as the valedictorian of his class, he moved to Connecticut to attend Wesleyan University. While there, he earned a bachelor of arts degree in American studies, and he met graphic designer and illustrator Lisa Brown. The two started dating.

Handler and Brown married in 1998 while Brown was attending graduate school in New York. At the

While living in New York, Handler struggled to get his first book, *The Basic Eight,* published.

time, Handler was struggling to get his first novel published. For money, he played piano in cocktail bars and for dance classes. Finally, after being rejected by thirty-five editors, Handler found a publisher for his first book. *The Basic Eight,* a story for adult readers, was published in 1999. Handler's next book, also for adults, came out in 2000. This one, entitled *Watch Your Mouth,* actually made it onto the best-seller lists. By this time the first two Lemony Snicket books had already come out. They too quickly became hits.

When asked about the success of his books, Handler says he is surprised at the amount of recognition he has received. "I always thought that I would be a very, very minor but perhaps well-thought-of writer,"[3] he says. To this day, he remains surprised by his fame.

Chapter Two

The Birth of Lemony Snicket

When Daniel Handler began using the name Lemony Snicket, he never dreamed it would one day be famous. He started using the name while doing research for his first two adult books. He did not want his real name to end up on mailing lists, so he used the name Lemony Snicket when requesting information. (In interviews he has not revealed where this name came from.) People have pointed out to him that the name sounds very similar to the Disney character Jiminy Cricket. Handler assures readers that the rhyming names is purely an accident. Jiminy Cricket, he says, "is exactly the kind of overly moralistic, cheerful narrator who I despise."[4]

Lemony Snicket is best known as the narrator and author of A Series of Unfortunate Events. He officially entered the publishing world as the **nom de plume** of Daniel Handler in 1999. Handler's editor friend Susan Rich had approached him about writing children's books for HarperCollins publishers. Handler was intrigued by his friend's proposal. He knew that she hoped he would write something a little untraditional, something different from other modern children's books.

In writing A Series of Unfortunate Events, Handler creates the kinds of books that he would have enjoyed reading as a child. When he began writing the series, however, he made a point of *not* reading any current children's books because he did not want to be influenced by other writers. Even without reading other children's books, Handler knew what kinds of books he did *not* want to write. He did not want to write books with syrupy-sweet beginnings that promised a safe, happy reading experience. And he especially did

Handler's central characters in the 2004 movie version of A Series of Unfortunate Events constantly found themselves in dangerous and frightening situations.

These fans are waiting anxiously to have Lemony Snicket sign their copies of *The Grim Grotto,* the eleventh book in the unhappy series.

not want to write books with heavy-handed moralistic messages.

When thinking about his stories, Handler always wonders about all the horrible things that could happen to his characters. "Most books, it seems to me, have at least the threat of something dastardly happening," Handler says, "so it just seems entirely natural to me that if you want a plot to be interesting, then terrible things have to be on the horizon."[5]

The Baudelaire kids have more than their fair share of awful experiences. Their parents are killed in a fire, they suffer the continuing torment of Count Olaf, and they encounter deadly leeches and toe-pinching crabs during their adventures. They are forced to work in a sinister lumber mill and a scary hospital, and they find themselves exploring a dangerous underwater cave. Their only friends are kidnapped, and any kindly caretakers they meet are murdered or mysteriously disappear. And in every book, the adults in their lives are unable to protect them from the evil schemes of Count Olaf.

Handler's Childhood

Handler explains that when he was a child, some of the adults around him seemed a little scary. Even around adults who were nice, Handler says,

> I think I had a sense that the world was not in my control, that decisions were being made on my behalf by people much taller than me who were unlikely to pay attention no matter how many times I repeated my question. And I think that I'm not alone in that perception, and that's why there's so many evil and/or inept adults in my books.[6]

The themes in Handler's books are also influenced by the childhood experiences of his father. Lou Handler lived in Germany as a child. His family was Jewish. They fled Germany in 1938 to escape Nazi persecution. While some Jews (like Handler's father) escaped, 6 million Jews were killed during what is now known as the **Holocaust.** This family history has found its way into Handler's work. He says, "The idea that the world could suddenly go very wrong—and that it had no bearing on what sort of person you were—sunk in pretty early. It's affected my politics and my writing and my life."[7]

Handler poses with a sketch of the evil Count Olaf (left), played by actor Jim Carrey (right) in the 2004 film.

Daniel Handler Has Fun as Lemony Snicket

While Handler's themes may spring from serious events, he seems to be having lots of fun with the mysterious Lemony Snicket. In the novels, Snicket is known as the peculiar author and narrator who is obsessed with researching and reporting on the lives of the Baudelaire orphans. He is tight-lipped about his own past and refuses to be photographed. He also drops hints about being wanted by the authorities and about his love for a mysterious woman named Beatrice, to whom he dedicates each book.

Knowing that his readers want to learn more about the life of Lemony Snicket, Handler does his best to

As Lemony Snicket's representative, Handler enjoys joking around with the kids who come to his book signings.

Children of all ages come to Snicket's book signings, hoping to learn more about the mysterious author.

thicken the fog of mystery surrounding Snicket. In public appearances, Handler often claims to be Lemony Snicket's representative. Handler often shows up wearing a black cape and carrying an accordion. He has been known to tell his audience that Snicket would not be able to attend the event because he had met with an unfortunate accident. At one such appearance, he told fans Snicket had been stung in the armpit by an exotic bug, and he brought it in a glass as proof. "I tell them this should teach them a lesson," Handler says. "Never raise your hand, especially not in class."[8]

Some of Snicket's fans leave these appearances disappointed that Snicket himself did not appear. But many readers see through the charade and realize that Handler is the real Lemony Snicket. During these appearances, Handler often sings gloomy ballads about the Baudelaire orphans while playing his accordion. He also encourages members of the audience to run around as though they were being chased by Count Olaf. Then they play dead, as though they had been caught.

Another way Handler has had fun with the Lemony Snicket **persona** is through writing *Lemony Snicket: The Unauthorized Autobiography.* The autobiography does more to enhance the mysteries surrounding Snicket than to solve them. More of a scrapbook of sorts, the book includes fake newspaper clippings, diary entries, and blurry photographs of people who may or may not be Lemony Snicket. Also included are quotes from other children's books and possible clues to the outcome of the Unfortunate Events series.

Handler's antics as Lemony Snicket and *Lemony Snicket: The Unauthorized Autobiography* have added to the author's popularity. But the books in A Series of Unfortunate Events themselves are still the main attraction.

Chapter Three

A World of Words and Ideas

The Bad Beginning, the first book in A Series of Unfortunate Events, sets the tone for the whole series. It begins with a warning to readers: "If you are interested in stories with happy endings, you would be better off reading some other book. In this book, not only is there no happy ending, there is no happy beginning and very few happy things in the middle."[9]

The author goes on to explain that misfortune will follow the Baudelaire orphans wherever they go. Each book finds the orphans under the care of new adult guardians who are unable to protect them from harm. As a result, the three siblings find themselves very much alone in the world.

The orphans' misadventures are exaggerated to help create exciting plots for the books but share a common theme. They remind young readers that bad things can happen, things that adults are not always able to fix. Having already lost both of their parents in a fire, for example, the Baudelaire children have to face the reality of

In this scene from the movie, the Baudelaire children are sent to live with the creepy Count Olaf after their parents die in a fire.

death again when their beloved Uncle Monty dies in Snicket's second book, *The Reptile Room*. As the narrator of the scene, Snicket tries to put the children's feelings about death in perspective for young readers. He explains how the death of someone we know comes as a surprise even though we all know that everyone dies eventually.

> It is like walking up the stairs to your bedroom in the dark, and thinking there is one more stair than there is. Your foot falls down, through the air, and there is a sickly moment of dark surprise as you try and readjust the way you thought of things. [10]

In passages like this one, real feelings merge with fictional events.

Reality merged with fiction yet again after the real-life terrorist attack on New York's World Trade Center on September 11, 2001. During this scary and confusing time, Handler reports that Lemony Snicket received many letters from his young fans. Even though the series is not set in any identifiable place (such as New York), they worried that the Baudelaire children may have been harmed in the attack on New York. They also wondered if Count Olaf might be a terrorist. Snicket's readers were thinking about evil and where it comes from, Handler says.

After the 2001 terrorist attacks on the United States, some Snicket fans began to wonder if Count Olaf might actually be terrorist.

Concerns About the Books

Reviews of A Series of Unfortunate Events indicate that both young and old readers alike are enjoying the Baudelaires' mishaps. Most of the public response to Snicket's work has been favorable. Some has not. Some people

Handler gives public readings across the United States, to the delight of both young and old readers.

find the stories to be too dark and upsetting for young readers.

One school in Decatur, Georgia, had a different objection to Snicket's work. School administrators there asked Snicket to cancel his scheduled visit after they discovered that Count Olaf uses the word *damn* in the book *The Reptile Room*. The school later banned the books from the campus. Snicket was not upset, but he was surprised. The offending word in the text actually followed a discussion about not using such strong words. The author explains that "its use was precipitated by a long discussion of how one should never say this word, since only a villain would do so vile a thing! This is exactly the lily-liveredness of children's books that I can't stand."[11]

Other readers have expressed concern that Count Olaf is too evil for children's books or that Snicket may be teaching immoral lessons. One reader, for example, was upset that in one scene Snicket tells readers that it is sometimes necessary to tell lies.

New Words

Despite this criticism, many teachers, librarians, and parents praise the Snicket books. One of the things they like about them, aside from the stories, is the author's use of language. As the narrator of the series, Snicket often uses big words when telling the Baudelaires' story. Many of these words are above the reading level of the series' readers, and Snicket knows it. Unfamiliar words can often turn readers away from books, but Snicket makes these words fun by humorously defining them within the novels.

As narrator, Snicket often interrupts suspenseful scenes to explain the elements of writing. In *The Reptile Room*, for example, Snicket breaks into the story to define *dramatic irony*. He defines this term as that sinking feeling readers have when they know something awful is going to happen to a character, but the character does not know it yet. He also interrupts his storytelling to define **clichés**, which are overused phrases, such as "dead as dirt" or "skinny as a rail." He pauses again to explain the use of **colloquial expressions**, such as "speak of the devil" and other similar phrases found in everyday speech.

Handler says he does not plan ahead for such lessons or explanations. He just uses words he likes and hopes that readers enjoy learning new words as they follow the Baudelaire orphans' adventures.

Snicket's Allusions

In addition to introducing readers to new words, Snicket's books are full of **allusions** to other books, popular culture, and even politics. One example of a literary allusion is Snicket's use of the name Mr. Poe as the orphans' banker and the man in charge of finding caretakers for the children. His name is a reference to Edgar Allan Poe, the nineteenth-century American writer best known for his horror stories and detective tales. Even Snicket's youngest readers are able to catch some of these allusions. Most, however, are intended for adult fans who have more experience as readers. "I know a lot of younger readers won't pick up all the references now," Handler says, "but I love the idea that

Lemony Meanings

Aura of Menace:
Having an aura of menace is like having a pet weasel, because you rarely meet someone who has one and when you do it makes you want to hide under the coffee table.

Brace Yourself:
The expression "brace yourself," as I'm sure you know, does not mean to take some metal wiring and rivets and other orthodontic materials and apply them to your own teeth in order to straighten them. The expression means "get ready for something that will probably be very difficult."

Fate:
Fate is like a strange, un-popular restaurant, filled with odd waiters who bring you things you never ask for and don't always like.

Taking One's Chances:
Taking one's chances is like taking a bath, because some-times you end up feeling comfortable and warm, and sometimes there is something terrible lurking around you that you cannot see until it is too late and you can do nothing else but scream and cling to a plastic duck.

Uncle Monty warns the Baudelaire kids not to let the Virginian Wolfsnake near the typewriter, an allusion to writer Virginia Woolf.

years from now they'll be sitting in lit class and the other shoe will drop."[12] One fan has even created a Web site that notes the many literary and cultural allusions in the series.

Chapter Four

Handler and Snicket: Where Are They Now?

I n October 2003, Handler and his wife welcomed their first-born child, a baby boy, to their family. The three live comfortably in a roomy Victorian house in San Francisco. Like the house of his childhood, Handler's home is warm and inviting, according to one interviewer. It is not the kind of creepy house fans might imagine. "I think some people expect me to be a little spookier than I am,"[13] Handler says with a laugh.

When Handler's child was born, his tenth book in A Series of Unfortunate Events, *The Slippery Slope*, was nearing publication. Book eleven, *The Grim Grotto*, was published in October 2004 and almost immediately made it onto the *Wall Street Journal*'s weekly best-seller list. Only two books remain until the series is complete.

Unfortunate Events at a Theater Near You

In the meantime, Handler has been working on other projects. One is a book of short stories for adults. He has also been busy over the last couple of years with film projects. He wrote the screenplay for the first of these projects, which is a movie for adult viewers.

Handler wrote the screenplay for the low budget film, *Rick,* which was released in October 2004.

Daniel Handler poses with producer Walter Parks at the Los Angeles premiere of *A Series of Unfortunate Events*.

Handler's second film project, released in December 2004, is a movie version of A Series of Unfortunate Events. The movie mostly covers events from the first book, but it also includes scenes from later books in the series.

In this way it differs from another well-known children's book series that has become an equally popular series of movies. The Harry Potter movies, based on the books by J.K. Rowling, have tried to remain faithful to each book in the series. This was not a goal in the Lemony Snicket movie. Like Rowling, however, Handler has had some involvement in the movie. He

Handler poses with actresses Meryl Steep and Emily Browning, who play strong female characters in the movie.

originally hoped to write the movie version, or screen-play, of his books. That job proved more difficult than he imagined. After the eighth draft, he enlisted the help of a professional screenwriter.

Although he did not have complete control over the movie script, Handler reports that he is pleased with the casting and the sets. He is a little wary, however, about how movie versions of books can sometimes change authors' characters. After viewing *Harry Potter and the Sorcerer's Stone,* for example, Handler was an-noyed at the film's portrayal of J.K. Rowling's character Hermione Granger.

He remembers Hermione as being smart and appre-ciated for it in Rowling's book. In the film version, he said he noticed that every time Hermione said something smart, the camera would pan over to catch a shot of the boys rolling their eyes. He explains, "If you are a girl seeing this movie—and you're the kind of girl who is always reading a lot, learning lots of facts—then the lesson you're going to get from this film is that somehow, that is not the appealing and acceptable way for a girl to behave."[14]

Handler believes there are not enough good female characters in children's books and movies. In his own series, he says, he wanted to make his girl characters special. Violet, with her skills at inventing, and even baby Sunny, knowing just when to use her sharp teeth to get out of tough situations, both do more than many other girl characters he has come across.

Count Olaf welcomes the Baudelaire kids into his home in this movie scene. Handler likes how the movie brings his characters to life.

While Handler is unhappy with the portrayal of Hermione in the Harry Potter movies, he is happy about the success of the Harry Potter novels. He feels that the media attention that children's literature gets from both Rowling's series and his own shows a new appreciation for young readers. The more media attention these series get, the more likely other publishers will be willing to take chances on other new writers.

Thinking of the Future

With the appearance of the movie version of A Series of Unfortunate Events, Handler has had to think about another side of the business. Toys, action figures, board and video games, lunch boxes, backpacks, and clothing are a common offshoot of successful kids' movies.

Three cast members from the film sing a Christmas carol at a 2004 tree lighting celebration in Los Angeles.

Readers hope that Daniel Handler will dream up many more unfortunate events for the Baudelaire orphans.

Handler is not sure how he feels about such merchandising. On the one hand, he says, he does not want to see his books tied in with fast-food giveaways. On the other hand, he understands that his young readers may want to play with toys and games connected with the books and movie. He feels this kind of play is positive because it encourages children to use their imaginations. "A movie like *Star Wars* seems over-merchandised," he explains, "but it would really be impossible to overemphasize how much fun I had when I was a kid playing with all the 'Star Wars' characters and making up my own stories and I think becoming a storyteller rose out of that kind of play."[15]

And being a storyteller is what Handler does best. He does it so well that his Lemony Snicket character has truly come to life. As he concludes his research into the lives of the Baudelaire orphans, Snicket's readers can only hope for him the same as he has predicted for his series. As he says, the "ending that is on the horizon will be happier than some, but less happy than others."[16]

Notes

Introduction: The Most Dreadful Books
1. Lemony Snicket, *The Hostile Hospital*. New York: HarperTrophy, 2001.

Chapter One: The Real Lemony Snicket
2. Quoted in *Publishers Weekly*, "Oh, Sweet Misery," May 29, 2000, p. 42.
3. Quoted in Sarah Putt, "A Major Writer for the Minor Set," http://xtramsn.co.nz/home.

Chapter Two: The Birth of Lemony Snicket
4. Quoted in Daniel Handler and Terry Gross, *Fresh Air*, National Public Radio, WHYY, Philadelphia, December 10, 2001.
5. Quoted in Handler and Gross, *Fresh Air*.
6. Quoted in Handler and Gross, *Fresh Air*.
7. Quoted in *The Writer*, "Miscellany: Authors Explain Themselves," February 2004, p. 10.
8. Quoted in *Publishers Weekly*, "Oh, Sweet Misery," p. 42.

Chapter Three: A World of Words and Ideas
9. Lemony Snicket, *The Bad Beginning*. New York: HarperTrophy, 1999, p. 1.
10. Lemony Snicket, *The Reptile Room*. New York: HarperTrophy, 1999, pp. 96–97.
11. Quoted in *Publishers Weekly*, "Oh, Sweet Misery," p. 42.

12. Quoted in Vicki Haddock, "Shivers Under the Covers: On the Lemony Snicket Publishing Phenomenon," *San Francisco Chronicle*, May 23, 2002.

Chapter Four: Handler and Snicket: Where Are They Now?

13. Quoted in James Sullivan, "He's Having a Baby," *Book*, November/December 2003, p.52.
14. Quoted in David Templeton, "Boy's World," *MetroActive*, November 15, 2001.
15. Quoted in Handler and Gross, *Fresh Air.*
16. Quoted in Lisa Leff, "Fortune Smiles on Creator of 'A Series of Unfortunate Events,'" *Miami Herald (Herald.com)*, October 15, 2004.

Glossary

allusions: Indirect references to something else in a work of literature. A character's name may be an allusion to another character in a different author's novel, for instance.

clichés: Overused phrases or expressions.

colloquial expressions: Words that can be found in everyday, informal speech.

Holocaust: The systematic persecution and murder of millions of Jewish people and others in concentration camps in Europe during World War II.

nom de plume: A made-up name that authors use when they do not want to reveal their true identities to readers.

persona: A fictional character or identity.

For Further Exploration

Nonfiction Books and Articles

Louis Gresh, *The Truth Behind* A Series of Unfortunate Events: *Eyeballs, Leeches, Hypnotism and Orphans— Exploring Lemony Snicket's World.* New York: Griffin, 2004. This companion guide to Lemony Snicket's A Series of Unfortunate Events provides facts on everything from handwriting analysis and forgery to killer leeches and hypnosis. There are quizzes, anecdotes, lessons on building hot air balloons, and much more.

Time for Kids, "He Tells Terrible Tales," April 27, 2001. This short article includes an in-character interview with Lemony Snicket, who maintains that people should not read any of his books.

Fiction by Lemony Snicket (in Series Order)

The Bad Beginning. New York: HarperTrophy, 1999. The first book introduces readers to Violet, Klaus, and Sunny just as they learn their parents have been killed in a fire. They are sent to the conniving Count Olaf, who plots to inherit their fortune.

The Reptile Room. New York: HarperTrophy, 1999. The Baudelaire orphans are sent to live with their kind, snake-loving Uncle Monty, who dies when Count Olaf arrives on the scene.

The Wide Window. New York: HarperTrophy, 2000. Violet, Klaus, and baby Sunny are sent to live with

Aunt Josephine, a phobic grammar expert, whose house on a cliff overhangs the deadly leeches in Lake Lachrymose.

The Miserable Mill. New York: HarperTrophy, 2000. The Baudelaire orphans wind up working for coupons (to pay for food and basic necessities) in a sinister lumber mill. Violet suspects Count Olaf of hypnotizing Klaus.

The Austere Academy. New York: HarperTrophy, 2000. At Prufrock Preparatory School, Violet and Klaus suffer boredom at the hands of their teachers. They also have to contend with toe-pinching crabs, ceiling fungus, and Count Olaf.

The Ersatz Elevator. New York: HarperTrophy, 2001. The Baudelaire children are adopted by a wealthy, shallow couple who live in a seventy-one-bedroom apartment in a high-rise with no elevators.

The Vile Village. New York: HarperTrophy, 2001. The Baudelaire orphans are adopted by an entire town governed by crows. They are forced to do all the village chores until they are falsely imprisoned for the murder of Count Olaf.

The Hostile Hospital. New York: HarperTrophy, 2001. On the run from the Vile Village, Violet, Klaus, and Sunny hide amidst the V.F.D. (Volunteers for Fighting Disease) and end up in a very unhealthful hospital indeed.

The Carnivorous Carnival. New York: HarperTrophy, 2002. Still on the run as suspected murderers, the

Baudelaire orphans masquerade as freaks in a carnival in order to hide from the sinister Count Olaf.

Lemony Snicket: The Unauthorized Autobiography. New York: HarperTrophy, 2002. This cryptic scrapbook of newspaper clippings, diary entries, and blurry photographs is a must-have for those curious about the narrator of A Series of Unfortunate Events.

The Slippery Slope. New York: HarperTrophy, 2003. In the Mortmain Mountains, Violet and Klaus must rescue Sunny from the clutches of Count Olaf. They meet an intelligent, well-read friend who helps them.

The Grim Grotto. New York: HarperTrophy, 2004. The Baudelaire orphans travel in a battered submarine to the Gorgonian Grotto, a dangerous underwater cave.

Web Sites

LemonySnicket.com (www.lemonysnicket.com). This is Daniel Handler's official Web site for Lemony Snicket. It features biographical information on both Handler and Snicket, it lists the author's books, and it provides excerpts and character sketches from A Series of Unfortunate Events.

Lemony Snicket Readalikes (www.mesalibrary.org/teens/readinglists/lemonysnicket.asp). This Web site provides a sizable listing of books young readers might enjoy if they like Lemony Snicket's A Series of Unfortunate Events. The list is maintained by the City of Mesa Library in Mesa, Arizona.

Quidditch.com's Incomplete Guide to Lemony Snicket Allusions (www.quidditch.com/lemony%20 snicket.htm). This fun Web site is both entertaining and educational for Lemony Snicket fans. It provides a book-by-book listing and explanation of the literary and cultural allusions abounding in the Unfortunate Events series.

Index

About the Author

Hayley Mitchell Haugen holds master's degrees in English and creative writing, and she is currently working on a PhD in American literature at Ohio University. She teaches creative writing and composition at the college level and has written numerous nonfiction books for teens and children published by Greenhaven Press, Lucent Books, and KidHaven Press.